T0130272

# THE
# "WHAT IF..."
# BOOK

*JOURNEY TO A JOYFUL LIFE...*

....................................................

## STEVEN MCMANUS

Balboa Press books may be ordered through booksellers or by contacting:

Balboa Press
A Division of Hay House
1663 Liberty Drive
Bloomington, IN 47403
www.balboapress.com
1 (877) 407-4847

ISBN: 978-1-9822-2776-0 (sc)
ISBN: 978-1-9822-2777-7 (e)

Library of Congress Control Number: 2019906848

Print information available on the last page.

Balboa Press rev. date: 06/07/2019

BALBOA
PRESS
A DIVISION OF HAY HOUSE

# The "WHAT IF..." BOOK

# Mom and Renée

# DEDICATION

This book is dedicated to the two most important women in my life, my Mom Barbara, and my wife Renée.

My older brother Mark, younger sister Linda and I were lucky enough to have a stay at home mom. We grew up in a small suburban town called Livermore, in the booming state of California.

Mom was always there when we came home from school, to share all that we learned and accomplished in our little lives. Mom's enthusiastic and positive listening skills allowed me to relive every story I told, with the feeling Mom was right there watching with a big smile as it happened. Mom's love for all of us continued till her death in 2018. Here's a poem I wrote for Mom the day of her death.

**Mom**
**Oct 11, 1925 - June 10, 2018**

*My biggest fan has died,*
*But don't feel bad for me...*

*We laughed together for 60 years...*
*We drank coffee and talked about children and life*

*Mom loved and accepted the good and not so good in me...*
*Provided an ear and heart on demand*

*We had a special connection where nothing could hide...*
*So nothing did*

*To be loved for who you are, is priceless...*
*Thank you, Mom...I love you too*

I met my wife Renée in a hospital we worked in while I was going to college. It was love at first sight for me, but it took a while and some prodding from Renée before we actually went on a date. The rest is history. To be married to, loved and accepted by a beautiful nurse is a fantasy for some, but a reality for me. Here's a poem I surprised Renée with on our wedding day. I still feel the same way about Renée today.

*Wedding Poem*
*May 5, 1985*

*I was content,*
*Till I saw her smile...*
*Beckoning to me...*
*Like a blazing campfire on a cold night...*

*When I spoke to her*
*I saw myself, reflected in the mirrors of her kind eyes...*
*And when I touched her,*
*I felt the rays of the sun, vibrating thru me,*
*Awakening me from a deep sleep*

*When I need her, she's there*
*As the sun is there for the coming dawn...*
*And when she needs help,*
*She allows me into her secret place,*
*Where I can feel important in her life...*

*I was content, till I saw her smile...*
*Content to sleep, until Renée*

# The Great Pyramid of Giza

# Epigraph

"You don't have to search for your path, it comes to you, moment by moment..." *Janet Myatt*

# Sphinx and Great Pyramid of Giza

# PREFACE

It was a cool, brisk, nearly pitch-black morning in Cairo Egypt as fifteen of us boarded a luxury tour bus. The air was filled with new day smells as we made our way to the mighty Sphinx. We were suddenly stopped at a security check point by Egyptian army personnel. Conversations between bus drivers, guides and authorities broke the silence. Our attention was soon stolen as we watched packs of dogs, horses and chickens roam free through the streets. Soon we arrived, finding our way to the huge timeless structure with the help of our cellphone lights.

We were encouraged to walk around and feel the wonder as we mingled within this historical space, waiting for one of the highlights of our trip. A channeled message from an Egyptian collective known as Min, compliments of a talented and blessed Psychic Medium Jennifer Starlight, would soon begin.

As we all took our places against the inner arms of the Sphinx, with Jennifer between us under the enormous head, channeling began. Messages of unity, love, merging of souls, lights and hearts from Min filled the air.

After 10 minutes or so passed, Min asked for questions. Silence screamed as I fumbled for a question. I imagined others felt the same way I did. I wanted to take advantage of this sacred moment, but the fear that my question was too weak, or silly was holding me back. Relief was felt as others broke the silence and questions and answers started to flow. Now my fear changed to, what if I don't get a chance to ask my question? During a slight pause, I blurted out my question:

    *Me*: "Min, could you give me help to see things more through God's eyes?" Pause, *Stupid question!* Ran through my mind.

    Min: We will say to you, you need to start seeing things more through your own eyes, because you are God, it's impossible for you not to be. The impossible part is the programming you've been given about God. Do you understand what we say?"

    *Me*: "Yes." *Well kind of,* I thought.

    Min: "The powerless ones have given you stories that make it impossible for you to believe or receive the fact that you are God in its trillions and trillions of forms. If you wish to see through your own inner God, drop your awareness into your heart brother. That is how you will see through God's eyes, and everybody you come across, focus upon their heart, and there will be God realization. It is very, very simple."

*Me*: "Great!" came out of my mouth, *ok that wasn't such a bad question* I thought.

Min: "Do we have permission to talk to your soul because it is screaming at us?"

*Me*: "Yes please" *Oh boy, this is getting exciting!*

Min: "All right, let us have a look. Interesting, this is going to sound like a cliché brother, however, why have you not written that book?"

Laughter crept into the holy moment.

*Me*: "Which one?" sheepishly came out of my mouth.

Min: "Which one, you have several in mind?"

*Me*: "Yes, I'm just ah…"

Min: "Procrastinating!"

*Me*: "Yes, thank you."

Min: "All right, this is your soul talking to us. The first paragraph of your book is going to be, "The day, the morning I stood at the Sphinx and the rest will come…"

Me: "Ah, ok thank you!" *Wow how unexpected* I thought.

Min: "You will get the inspiration and we look forward to reading it, because it is going to become a passion, it is going to overtake you brother for a little while, but that is a good thing."

Min: Because this father is looking for many ways to express itself and if each of you here give it permission to work through you in unique ways, your lives will become absolutely extraordinary. So, do you give this being permission to work through you?"

Everyone: "Yes!"

# ACKNOWLEDGMENTS

So many people to acknowledge. I'll start with my Mom, Dad, brother Mark, sister Linda and wife Renée, who gave me a behind the scene look at real love and happiness. My dog Casey should be mentioned as no one could love me as much. Not even me, but I'm working on it.

**Authors that have influenced me and this book through the years are listed below:**

Edgar Cayce

Deepak Chopra

Paulo Coelho

April Crawford (*VERONICA*)

Mike Dooley

Kahlil Gibran (*The Prophet*)

Thich Nhat Hanh

Trudy Harris RN (*Glimpses of Heaven*)

Tyler Henry

Esther Hicks

Matt Kahn

Raymond Moody (*Life after Life*)

Janet Myatt

Caroline Myss

Helen Schucman and William Thetford (*A Course in Mircles*)

Jane Roberts (*Seth Speaks*)

Jennifer Starlight

Eckhart Tolle

Neale Donald Walsch (*Conversations with God*)

William Paul Young (*The Shack*)

# The Sphinx

# INTRODUCTION

The day, the morning I stood at the Sphinx, was the day this book was born. This book had been swimming around in my head for years, telling me it wasn't ready yet, it wasn't good enough, no one would want to read it, why should anyone listen to me, I'm not more important than anyone else and the thousand other excuses we all hear that hold us in a procrastination pattern.

November 12, 2018 was the day Psychic Medium Jennifer Starlight, along with her channeled Egyptian consciousnesses Min, startled me with the words "Why have you not written that book?" Well here it is, and with the blessings of God, may the truth in it impact your life in joyous and loving ways.

# GOD

*If there is a God*
*God is part of everything*
*Which includes us too*

# CHAPTER 1

**God, Heaven and Earth**

What if ... there is a God

    ... God is in everything, including us

    ... we are all connected to everyone and everything through God

    ... we are a part of God

    ... others are a part of God

    ... God exchanges unconditional love with us

    ... we all come from a place called heaven

    ... there is only perfect love in heaven

    ... life on earth is where we go to experience imperfect love

    ... life on earth is a place to experience and understand imperfection

# LOVE

*Love is powerful*
*Love is also so gentle*
*Love is what we need*

# CHAPTER 2

**Love and Drama**

What if ... the goal of life is to experience the power of love

... love makes every situation better

... responding with love is always the best response

... perfect spirits come to earth to experience imperfection

... life is like a play, and our spirits are the actors

... we choose the roles we play in our life's drama. Sometimes the hero, sometimes the villain, most times a little of both

... we write our own scripts as we play the characters we choose

... we forget we are playing roles in life's drama once we are born

... all of us earth actors reunite after we awaken from our life dream, and have an awards party in heaven

# CHOICE

*Choice is always ours*
*Our life reflects our choices*
*How does your day look?*

# CHAPTER 3

**Choice and Reflection**

What if ... we are always free to choose whatever we want in life

    ... choices not made by us, are made by another part of us and branch off a parallel life

    ... there are no wrong choices

    ... all possible choices are desired to be experienced by our Soul or higher self

    ... our choices in life, trigger karma

    ... things we do to others, are done to us

    ... our choices guide the experiences we receive

    ... we see ourselves in others

    ... others are a reflection of us

    ... our life is a reflection of us

    ... our life is a reflection of our thoughts, desires, beliefs and choices

# YOU

*Be good to yourself*
*Everything starts with you first*
*A good foundation*

# CHAPTER 4

**Love and Forgiveness**

What if ... we are here to give and receive love

      ... by loving ourself, we are loving others

      ... we find one thing to love about ourself today

      ... we find something to love about another today

      ... we find something to love about our life today

      ... we forgive ourself for not being perfect

      ... we forgive others for not being perfect

      ... not forgiving holds anger inside us

      ... anger held inside, causes disease

# IMPERFECTION

*Nothing is perfect*
*Imperfection allows growth*
*Up for the challenge?*

# CHAPTER 5

**Imperfection, Judgment and Acceptance**

What if ... no one on earth is perfect

    ... imperfection is a chance to grow

    ... we allow children to learn from mistakes

    ... everyone can learn best from their mistakes

    ... we continue to make the same mistakes until we learn

    ... all of us are still learning

    ... life is always teaching

    ... we don't judge ourselves and offer only love, acceptance and understanding

    ... we don't judge others and offer only love, acceptance and understanding

# SOULS

*What does our soul want?*
*To experience the Love*
*That's what I want too*

# CHAPTER 6

**Our Soul's Purpose**

What if ... we are here to fulfill our soul's purpose

   ... we can communicate with our soul

   ... every soul's purpose involves love

   ... our soul communicates through joy

   ... our positivity affects others

   ... our negativity affects others

   ... we notice things that went well today and feel gratitude

   ... we make gratitude part of our purpose

   ... we smile more today

# KINDNESS

*Love moves thru kindness*
*Kindness is Love in action*
*Catch it if you can*

# CHAPTER 7

**Kindness and Trust**

What if ... we do a random act of kindness today

... we do a random act of kindness everyday

... we are consistently kind to ourself

... we are consistently kind to others

... we practice responding with kindness

... we trust God

... we learn to trust ourself

... we trust the goodness in others

... hope is a prayer to strengthen trust

# CREATING

*What if we create*
*Thru thoughts, beliefs and desires*
*Let's be positive*

# CHAPTER 8

**Creating**

What if ... we create through love and joy

   ... we create through fear and anger

   ... every moment is a chance to create

   ... our thoughts create things

   ... all things that happen to us, are created by us

   ... we create from this moment with thoughts and desires

   ... we keep our thoughts joyous and positive in this moment

   ... all negative situations are opportunities to learn and grow

# LESSONS

*Life is our teacher*
*A lesson in every now*
*That's lots of lessons*

# CHAPTER 9

**Life's Lessons**

What if ... all moments contain lessons that we have the ability to learn

    ... experience is the best teacher

    ... there are no victims, only students

    ... every moment is a powerful gift

    ... every day provides opportunities for positive change

    ... we can change our world

# DEATH

*We will all pass on*
*The bus is always on time*
*We need not worry*

# CHAPTER 10

**Death, Angels and Grief**

What if ... we never die, we just awaken from our earth dream

    ... all pain leaves us during the awakening process

    ... life after death is wonderful beyond words

    ... we are greeted by loved ones when we pass

    ... no one is ever really hurt in life's dream

    ... our loved ones never leave us after they awaken from their dream

    ... we are never alone

    ... we have spirits, angels and guides that are always with us

    ... spirits, angels and guides are just another part of us

    ... We hear their guidance through thoughts, feelings and emotions

    ... we all grieve when loved ones die

    ... grieving is a testament to a loving relationship

    ... grieving turns to tribute when thoughts of loved ones passed, bring smiles

# MESSAGES

*We get messages*
*Whether we listen or not*
*Let's pay attention*

# CHAPTER 11

**Thought and Communication**

What if ... our spirits, angels and guides communicate through us to others

... God communicates to us through others

... we can connect with friends and loved ones who have passed with a thought

... we can communicate with friends and loved ones who have passed in our dreams

... we can connect to anyone with a thought

... we ask God for help when needed

... God always answers our prayers

# SOLUTIONS

*Sometimes we get stuck*
*There's no solution in sight*
*Look inside, it's there*

# CHAPTER 12

**Solutions**

What if ... God always provides solutions for us

    ... we can choose from many solutions

    ... all solutions have merit

    ... no solution is wrong

    ... we always choose what we need

    ... sometimes we need more lessons

    ... we choose to hurt others when we've been hurt

    ... no one wants to be hurt

    ... hurtful choices can cause anger

    ... forgiving hurtful choices releases us from anger

# FORGIVENESS

*Forgive and let go*
*Do not stay bound to pain*
*We deserve much more*

# CHAPTER 13

**Forgiveness and Acceptance**

What if ... forgiveness acknowledges experience understood

... forgiveness acknowledges we've all been hurt

... forgiveness releases us from negative thoughts

... forgiveness is a gift for us

... forgiveness is a powerful act of love to ourself

... forgiveness is a powerful act of love to others

... we can disagree with someone and still accept them

... we can accept someone with different beliefs

... no two people have the same beliefs

... unconditional love always includes acceptance and forgiveness

# PEACE

*Peace resides inside*
*Even when there is chaos*
*Peace is infectious*

# CHAPTER 14

**Peacefulness**

What if ... we can find a space for peace in chaos

    ... we can be calm in a chaotic world

    ... our calmness reduces stress in others

    ... stress in life hinders joy

    ... everyone wants more joy in their lives

    ... having gratitude, will bring more joy into our life

    ... practicing kindness brings more kindness into our life

    ... accepting our challenges will reduce anxiety in us

    ... peacefulness appears when anxiety leaves

# LIFE

*Life can get better*
*Life changes every moment*
*We are in control*

# CHAPTER 15

**Life Changes**

What if ... we can change our life for the better by doing the following:

Find something to love about yourself
Find something to love about another
Find something about your life to love
Forgive yourself for a mistake
Forgive another for a mistake
Smile at someone
Listen to your favorite music
Always thank someone that does something nice
Notice how positive acts affect others
Perform a random act of kindness
Give a family member a hug
Sing a song
Share your feelings with a family member
Share your feelings with a friend
Help someone in need
Learn from an experience
Hold a baby
Imagine something wonderful
Think about something that brings feelings of joy
Laugh with someone
Be grateful for something
Notice something good about someone
Thank God with a thought or prayer
Say a prayer for someone in need

# GOD IS LOVE

*We feel God on earth*
*Thru kindness and forgiveness*
*Acceptance and joy*

# CHAPTER 16

**Final Thoughts**

What if ... when we are kind, we experience God
       ... when we forgive, God's love is exchanged
       ... when we are at peace, we vibrate God's essence
       ... when we practice acceptance, we open God's heart and exchange grace
       ... when we trust, God responds with miracles
       ... when we bring love, God leaves footprints
       ... God is Love

Printed in the United States
By Bookmasters